The GLASSMAKERS

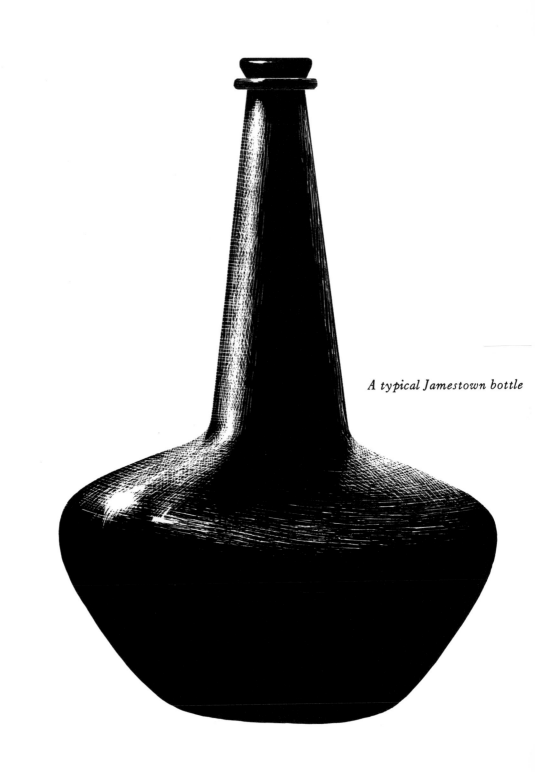

A typical Jamestown bottle

COLONIAL CRAFTSMEN

The
GLASSMAKERS

WRITTEN & ILLUSTRATED BY

Leonard Everett Fisher

BENCHMARK BOOKS

MARSHALL CAVENDISH
NEW YORK

Benchmark Books
Marshall Cavendish Corporation
99 White Plains Road
Tarrytown, New York 10591-9001

▬▬▬

Library of Congress Cataloging-in-Publication Data
Fisher, Leonard Everett.
The glassmakers / written & illustrated by Leonard Everett Fisher.
p.   cm. — (Colonial craftsmen)
Originally published: New York : Franklin Watts, 1964
Includes index.
Summary: Discusses the history, materials, and technique of glassmaking
in the American Colonies.
ISBN 0-7614-0477-5 (lib. bdg.)
1. Glass manufacture—Juvenile works. [1. Glass manufacture. 2. United States—
History—Colonial period, ca. 1600–1775.] I. Title.
II. Series: Fisher, Leonard Everett. Colonial craftsmen.
TP857.3.F48   1997   338.4'76661'097309032—dc20   96-16608   CIP   AC

▬▬▬

Printed and bound in the United States of America

1   3   5   6   4   2

Other titles in this series

═══════

═══════

For Richard, Jill, Douglas and Aaron

A Short History

O N MAY 13, 1607, ONE HUNDRED men and four boys founded the colony of Jamestown on the North American continent. One year later, they built America's first factory — a glasshouse, where glass was to be made.

The Jamestown adventurers were, for the most part, well-tailored English gentlemen. Their main purpose in making the trip to America was to find treasures of silver and gold. They did not plan to stay on American soil, once they had found wealth. England, in the seventeenth century, was a much better place to live happily rich forever after.

The London Company, sponsors of the venture, also had the idea of finding wealth. So did James I, King of England. The treasure sought by the Company and the Crown was not silver and gold, however. The sponsors and the king meant to help themselves to the vast supply of raw materials which they expected the colonists to find in America. They hoped to establish a permanent settlement where these raw materials would be turned into useful products. The products, cheaply made, would then be shipped

Jamestown

back to England for sale. The profits gained from such an operation were the treasure sought by the Company and King James.

Until they had a clear idea of the raw materials that might be found, the men of the London Company were unable to say what could be manufactured in the new colony. Captain John Smith, one of the voyagers, was convinced that the miles and tons of free sand on the Virginia beaches could be used to make glass. He suggested this to the men of the London Company, and they agreed. They sent eight Dutch and Polish glassmakers to Jamestown. Arriving in 1608, these glassmen immediately began to make bottles, which were then shipped to England for sale.

The little Jamestown factory was doomed, however. There were too many stylish gentlemen who would not work. There were not enough laborers who could work. And the Indians were no help at all. Besides, as the months passed and the hardships grew worse, the making of glass became more and more ridiculous to the settlers. Glass bottles were not yet a necessity of life to

*Italian glassmen
came secretly from Venice
to the New World*

anyone in the world, and especially not to those men and boys in the American wilderness. In 1609, America's first factory closed.

Nevertheless, the Company and the Crown still thought their scheme was a good one. Glass was not new. The Phoenicians had made it, five thousand years before. The early Egyptians had known how to make glass. The ancient Romans had made glass. Seventy-five years before the founding of Jamestown, even the Spaniards were making glass. If glass was not yet a necessity of life, the men of the London Company reasoned, it soon would become one. And so, once again, they tried to establish a very old craft in a very new world.

In 1621, a second Jamestown glass factory was started. This time, in addition to other products, the sponsors decided to make colored glass beads for trade with the Indians. But only Italian glassmen knew how to make them. Accordingly, the London Company, at great risk, smuggled six Italian glassmen and their beadmaking secrets out of Venice. Once the Italians arrived in Jamestown, the second factory began to produce bot-

tles and windowpanes for England, and glass beads for the Indians.

In 1622, the Indians attacked the settlement and massacred most of the inhabitants. Yet they did not destroy the factory. They wanted those beads! They allowed the glassmakers to continue — making beads only. This plan did not prove profitable to the Company or to the Crown, however, and in 1624 the second Jamestown factory closed.

Soon, other colonies began to appear along the eastern American shores. At the same time, glass was becoming popular in Europe. It was in demand for windows, tableware, chemical equipment, and optical instruments. To meet the need, small glasshouses were started in the New York, Massachusetts, and Philadelphia areas.

It was not until 1739 that the making of glass became a full-fledged industry in America. In that year, Caspar Wistar established a factory in Salem County, New Jersey. The Wistarberg Works, as it was known, thrived until 1781, the year when the American War for Independence ended. Wistar, and later his son, made a variety

The HISTORY

of products for both England and the colonies. They made bottles for snuff, spirits, mustard, and pickles; tubes, globes, jars, and retorts for chemists; and windowpanes for everyone.

The glass produced by the Wistarberg Works was made from the same raw materials and by the same methods as those used at Jamestown:

silica from sea and river sand,

soda from the sodium oxide found in salt deposits,

and lime from the calcium oxide provided by limestone.

Glass made from the blending of these ingredients was called "soda-lime" glass. It was dark in color and was not clear. It sounded dull when struck, and was inexpensive to make.

While the Wistarberg Works was toiling, Henry William Stiegel was experimenting. In 1765, Stiegel opened a glasshouse at Manheim, Pennsylvania. He owned everything in the town, including the orchestra. Everyone called him "Baron" Stiegel. The Manheim works produced glass of many shapes for many uses. It had a luster, a strength, and a beauty never before seen in American glass.

Liquor bottle

Snuff bottle

Creamer

It was not soda-lime glass, but a different kind, called "flint" glass. The basic ingredients used to make it were:

calcined flint, or flint powdered by heat,

soda,

and lead, or lead oxide.

Glass made with these ingredients was light in color, and clear. It sounded like a bell when struck, and was expensive to make.

Stiegel's business did not last as long as the Wistarberg Works had. He closed his factory in 1774, after operating for only nine years. But in that short time Henry William Stiegel achieved a quality of craftsmanship that brought world fame to colonial American glass.

Ale glass

Cologne bottle

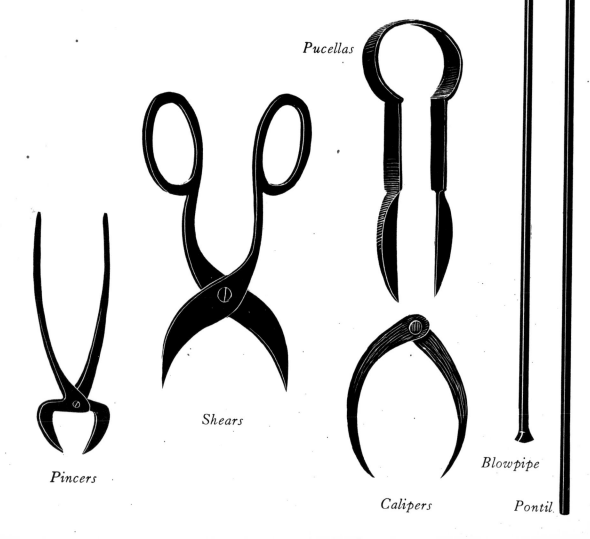

A GLASSMAKER'S TOOLS

How The
Glassmakers Worked

Battledore

Pucellas

Shears

Pincers

Calipers

Blowpipe

Pontil

THE VERY FIRST STEP IN GLASS-making was to build a proper furnace. The next step was to light a roaring fire inside. A very hot fire was necessary to melt and fuse the ingredients. It made no difference what type of glass was to be made — soda-lime or flint — there was no other way for a craftsman to make glass.

Each of the ingredients — silica, soda, and lime, or calcined flint, soda, and lead — was kept in an individual bin in a separate mixing room near the furnace. When the "gaffer," or master glassblower, was ready, he sent an assistant to the mixing room to prepare the glassmaking materials. There the ingredients were mixed together in certain proportions and were placed in a single fire-resistant clay pot called a "crucible." Added to the mixture were bits and pieces of glass of the same type and color as that which was to be made. These pieces of glass, called "cullet," helped to speed the fusion — the melting and blending together — of the ingredients.

The entire mixture, or "batch," contained in the crucible was brought to the furnace room and placed in the furnace. The roaring fire melted

A colonial glass factory

*Rolling molten glass
on a marver,
and gathering white-hot glass
on a blowpipe*

and fused the batch into one white-hot liquid mass, which was then ready to be shaped into a bottle or some other useful form.

During colonial times there were two methods of making hollow glasswares. In one method, the gaffer blew a glass bubble into a mold shaped exactly like the desired object. In the other method, the gaffer blew a glass bubble and created the desired shape without the use of a mold. This latter method was called the "offhand" method.

When the batch was properly fused, the gaffer and his assistants took their usual places near the furnace. The gaffer seated himself on a special bench, with his helpers in various positions around him. One assistant, the "fireman," made sure the fire stayed hot. Another assistant, called the "gatherer," began the delicate task of making a glass object.

The gatherer dipped a "blowpipe" — a long, hollow rod — into the crucible in the furnace. Out of it he lifted a small mass of white-hot melted glass. He then rolled the mass, called a "parison," on a "marver," or metal plate, to

The **TECHNIQUE**

smooth it out. The gatherer then took the parison, attached to the blowpipe, and handed it to the assistant blower. This helper placed the parison in an open-faced, rounded-out block of wood. Here he either continued to roll and smooth the parison, or else he blew a small bubble against the wood block to round off the bottom end of the parison.

The assistant blower then handed the blowpipe—with its smoothed-out, rounded-off parison — to the gaffer. The gaffer, after studying a sketch of the piece he was about to fashion, put the blowpipe to his mouth. Gently, evenly, he began to blow the parison into a larger and larger bubble.

When the bubble reached the size of the piece to be made, the gaffer was ready to shape it. By this time, the glass had cooled slightly and was very workable — and it took an expert like the gaffer to work it. The hot glass could be stretched and squeezed, twisted and flattened, cut and torn. It was like taffy candy! Since it was too hot to touch with his hands, the gaffer used a variety of tools to shape the glass bubble.

*The gaffer uses
the battledore to make a flat surface
on the bubble,
while the gatherer stands by
with a pontil*

The *TECHNIQUE*

He used:

a "battledore," a wood paddle for flattening,

"pucellas," a pair of tongs for twisting and stretching,

"shears," scissors for cutting and trimming,

"pincers," pliers for squeezing and stretching,

and "calipers," a device for measuring size.

If the glass became so cool and hard that it could not be shaped, an assistant placed it in the furnace through a special opening, and reheated it. After the glass had been reheated it was returned to the gaffer, who continued to shape it. The process of reheating was repeated as often as was necessary for the gaffer to finish the task of shaping.

Once the glass was shaped, the gatherer picked up a small amount of molten glass on the end of a long metal rod called a "pontil," or "punty." By means of the molten glass he connected the pontil to the bottom end of the newly shaped piece. The pontil, thus joined, then served as the working rod for holding the object, and the gaffer could cut away his blowpipe, leaving a rough opening.

*An assistant
takes the cool glassware
out of the lehr*

The *TECHNIQUE*

If the gaffer was making a simple bottle, he reheated the rough opening, trimmed it, smoothed it, and finished his job. He then gripped the bottle's neck with his pincers, and with one sharp rap from any handy tool he disconnected the pontil.

If the gaffer was fashioning a more complicated piece of glassware, which required handles and decorations, he left the pontil joined while he continued to stretch, squeeze, flatten, twist, and cut the piece. He added handles by fusing both ends of a molten string of glass to the decorated form, bending and shaping the handles as he saw fit. The trimmed piece was then detached from the pontil in the same manner as a bottle was. The small bits of glass that clung to the tools or fell to the floor were collected, washed, brought to the mixing room, and placed in the cullet bin.

An assistant then put the new glassware on a metal pan and placed it in a special oven called a "lehr" (pronounced *leer*). The lehr was usually long and narrow, and opened at both ends. One end was hotter than the other. The glass piece on

*The gaffer
blew this bubble of glass
into a hinged, two-piece mold*

the pan was inserted at the hot end of the oven and slowly pushed through until it reached the cool end. There it was removed, packed, and made ready for sale.

Pushing new glassware through the lehr was an important step in completing it. If glass cooled too rapidly and unevenly, as it must while the gaffer worked, it became too brittle. When glass was pushed through a lehr, it was reheated and allowed to cool slowly and evenly. This final process, which sometimes took days, gave strength to the glassware.

If, in the beginning, the gaffer had decided to use the mold method of fashioning hollow glass, he would have blown the bubble directly into a mold shaped like the piece he wished to make. The mold, rather than the gaffer, shaped the piece. Most molds were made in two pieces and were hinged. A mold like this could be opened easily, and the glass removed.

Some molds were miniatures of forms that were to be made larger. The gaffer blew a bubble into the small mold, which was then quickly opened while the gaffer continued to blow the

The *TECHNIQUE*

small hollow form into a larger one. During all the time the blowing continued, the glass maintained its original molded shape and proportions.

Windowpanes in colonial America also began with a glass bubble, but the manufacturing process was much different from that used to make hollow ware like bottles, jars, and globes. After the gaffer blew a small bubble and the bubble was connected to the pontil, he widened the rough opening left by the disconnected blowpipe. Having done this, he spun the pontil in the furnace until the side of the glass facing the flame flared out and flattened. He now had a bell-shaped glass.

The gaffer then fused another pontil to the inside top of the bell-like piece, removed the first pontil, and spun the glass again. This time, the entire piece flared and flattened into a disk. The gaffer then broke off the pontil from the center of the disk, leaving a bump. Because the bump was called a "crown," this method of making windowpanes was called the "crown" method. The windowpane was thickest at the crown. Little or no light passed through the disk at that point.

The TECHNIQUE

The TECHNIQUE

Certainly no one could see clearly through the crown, and he could hardly see through the outer edges of the windowpane, either. But that made no difference to the early colonists. Even a thick, dim piece of glass was better than oiled skin or cloth. And it was much better than no window at all, or an uncovered hole in the side of a house.

Later on, the glass disks were made larger. The colonists were then able to cut small rectangular pieces from the thinner outer edges. By joining these squared-off pieces of glass with leaden or wooden strips, the colonists provided themselves with better windows.

Some of the colonial glassmakers were very skillful with their tools. Others knew a great deal about different ingredients. Still others knew so much about the various manufacturing methods that they were able to improve them and devise new ones. All together, these master craftsmen created some of the most elegant glassware in the world. In so doing, they began a tradition of craftsmanship in American glass that is with us still and is admired everywhere.

Glassmaking Terms

BATCH — The mixture of raw ingredients for making glass.

BATTLEDORE — A flat wooden paddle used in shaping a molten glass object.

BLOWPIPE — A long, hollow rod used in shaping a glass object.

CALIPERS — A device used for measuring the size of a molten glass object.

CROWN — The thick bump left on a windowpane made by the early colonial method.

CRUCIBLE — A fire-resistant clay pot in which glassmaking ingredients were melted.

CULLET — Pieces of glass added to raw ingredients to speed fusion of the glassmaking materials.

FIREMAN — The assistant who kept the furnace hot.

GAFFER — A master glassblower.

GATHERER — The assistant who gathered the melted glass and began the task of shaping an object.

LEHR — A special oven used in strengthening glassware.

MARVER — The metal plate on which the parison was smoothed.

OFFHAND METHOD — A method of shaping a glass object by blowing, without the use of a mold.

PARISON — The mass of white-hot glass from which an object was shaped.

PINCERS — Pliers used for squeezing and stretching a molten glass object.

PONTIL — A long metal rod connected to a molten glass object to aid in holding it.

PUCELLAS — Tongs used for twisting and stretching a molten glass object.

PUNTY — A pontil.

SHEARS — Scissors for cutting and trimming a molten glass object.

Index

The text of this book has been composed on the linotype in Caslon 137. This face is derived from the great oldstyle cut by William Caslon of London in the early eighteenth century. Caslon types were used widely by American printers during the colonial period and even today it is considered to be "the finest vehicle for the conveyance of English speech that the art of the punch-cutter has yet devised."